A Ladybird Achievements Book
Series 601

Contents

THE STORY OF
Metals

by LESLIE AITCHISON,
D.Met. M.Sc.
*formerly Professor of
Industrial Metallurgy,
University of Birmingham*

with illustrations by
MARTIN AITCHISON

Publishers: Ladybird Books Ltd . Loughborough
© Ladybird Books Ltd (formerly Wills & Hepworth Ltd) 1971
Printed in England

In the beginning

Modern civilisation is based on metals and millions of tons are extracted from the surface of the Earth every year. How did they get there in the first place?

Many millions of years ago the Earth was much hotter than it is now. An outer layer, or *crust*, had formed of solid rock, but beneath this crust the temperature was far higher and rocks and metals were molten. The heavier substances sank to the centre of the Earth which even today is an inferno, largely of metals, at furnace heat and under tremendous pressure. Calculations suggest temperatures of 6000°C and pressures of 20,000 tons per square inch. (Over one million tons on an area the size of an open Ladybird book.)

Violent earthquakes and volcanic erruptions flung molten metals to the surface again to be trapped in hollows or spread over the Earth's crust, where they cooled and solidified. Nearly all these metals had combined with rock when molten to form metallic *ores*. Some metals did not combine with rocks and are known as *free* metals. Metallic ores or free metals could either be on the Earth's surface or in *veins* (seams) beneath it.

Finally all the waters of the Earth's oceans cooled, bringing centuries of torrential rain. The rain turned to steam on the hot rocks and formed clouds from which rain fell again and again. Rain and rivers eroded the surface of the Earth, wearing away the rocks to expose the veins of metal in some places and burying them under tons of soil in others.

The world slowly settled to the form and climate we know today and the metals awaited the advent of Man to discover and employ them.

(Above) Molten metal and rock pour together into a fissure
(Below) Centuries of rain erode rocks to expose a vein of metal

4

0 7214 0298 4

The early metal-workers

Millions of years passed before Man arrived on the Earth, and the very first metals which he encountered were probably *gold* and *copper*. Lumps of both these reddish-yellow metals could be picked up from the beds of streams where they had been washed free of earth and solids by the action of the water. To very primitive man these lumps of metal were merely stones like other pebbles. Perhaps his only use for a lump of gold would have been to throw it at a bird in the hope of a meal!

Later, when his intelligence was more developed, he began to experiment with these two metals. He discovered that gold and copper behaved quite differently from the flints he was so skilful at shaping. When he hammered flint it chipped or split, but the metals dented or altered shape. This is known as being *malleable*.

Gold is much softer than copper, so it is easier to hammer into shape. It is not very strong. A gold knife might look very fine but would not have been much use for skinning a bear, so from early times gold became the metal for ornaments. Copper is much harder; it would have been much more difficult for early man to shape, but the finished article was more durable.

Archaeologists have found evidence of early metal-work dating as far back as 10,000 BC. Such finds were made in the Middle East, where deposits of copper were most plentiful. This does not mean that this metal was easy to find, but that there were more deposits in the Middle East than other parts of the inhabited world.

Stone Age man throws a lump of gold

The application of heat to copper

Early man found that gold could be hammered almost endlessly to produce a required shape. Copper behaved quite differently. He found that as it was hammered it gradually hardened until it cracked. The early metal-workers (beaters) no doubt learned from bitter experience just how much they could alter the shape of a piece of copper without breaking it or causing it to become so brittle that the finished article was useless. Certainly they had ample time in which to gain experience and master their simple craft, because many centuries passed before it was discovered how to overcome the problem.

At some time between 9,000 and 4,500 BC it was found that if, after a certain amount of hammering, the copper was heated and then left to cool, it could be hammered again safely. So by heating the copper at intervals between hammering, far more elaborately shaped articles could be produced.

This discovery of the beneficial application of heat to metal is regarded as the first step in the science of metallurgy. The process is called *annealing*. The effect of the heat is to release the internal stresses and strains in the metal which have been set up by the hammering.

It is not known how this discovery was made. Possibly a brittle piece of copper was thrown into the fire, and afterwards it was noticed that the metal had softened.

Extracting copper from metal-bearing rock

No further development occurred until about 4,300 BC, when a most important discovery was made. This was the realization that copper could be extracted from metal-bearing rock (ore)—with which the metal had combined when the Earth cooled. If the ore was heated to a very high temperature, the compound of metal and rock was broken down, setting free the metal.

Much more copper then became available, because men did not have to rely on obtaining it only from those areas where it lay about on the surface of the ground.

As very frequently happens in science, this discovery was probably made accidentally by people engaged in something quite different. It is thought that in this case they were firing pottery. The best kilns of that time were capable of temperatures as high as 1200°C. This we know from a study of the remains of pottery of that time. It is probable that some metal-bearing rock found its way into the kiln, or the kiln was built of such rock. When the firing was complete, and the kiln cooled and was opened, the potter found not only his fired pots but solidified pools of copper. It may have happened many times before the significance was understood, but eventually it was realized that metals could be extracted from their ores by high temperatures. This process is known as *smelting*.

Other sources of high temperature may have served for the discovery, but the potter's kiln is the most probable.

A potter opens his kiln and finds a pool of copper

Two more metals—silver and lead

The discovery of smelting was made in the region of the Caspian Sea. Simple furnaces took the place of potters' kilns to 'win' copper from copper-ores, and the men who produced bright metal from dull rocks were regarded almost as magicians.

Merchant caravans were soon carrying copper to other countries of western Asia and then as far as Egypt, where copper articles have been found which were made long before the Great Pyramids were built.

Two new metals came into use at this time—about 4,000 BC. The first was *silver*, prized in those days as it is today, for its beauty, and used for ornaments. It was sometimes found 'free', lying around, as was gold, but was mostly smelted from ores. The second metal was *lead*, a dull heavy metal, soft and easily shaped into cups and beakers. Lead is never found 'free'; it has always been smelted from ore.

During the next 1,000 years the knowledge of the four metals so far known—gold, copper, silver and lead—spread to other lands. Troy (home of Helen), near the Dardanelles, was the chief centre of trade and from there goods were carried by boat into Europe. The River Danube provided a highway deep into the continent, and the traders' boats also took metal goods to all countries around the Mediterranean. Eventually they reached Britain, and the art of smelting and metal working became known in this country.

Quite early in the history of metal the process of *casting* was used to shape metal. Clay moulds were made of the required shape and molten metal poured in. When it was cold and hard it was removed; objects such as arrow-heads could be made quickly and needed only a minimum of beating and grinding to finish them.

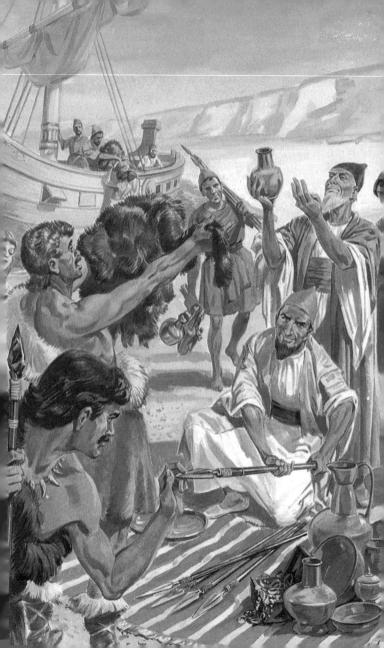

The importance of tin and the production of bronze

Although metals had been worked for about 7,000 years, only gold, silver, copper and lead were known before 2,500 BC. Then the fifth metal was discovered—*tin*. This is a soft, whitish metal (not to be confused with 'tin-cans') and at first was not considered to be of much value. However, as the result of another important metallurgical discovery, tin suddenly became highly prized. It was found that if tin and copper were melted together, a new metal was produced—almost twice as hard and strong as copper. This new metal was what we now call *bronze*, and it was the first *alloy*. An alloy is a metal made by combining other metals— a 'man-made' metal.

Various proportions of the two metals produced different qualities in the bronze. Most early metal-workers used about eight parts of copper to one of tin. Because weapons made of bronze were harder and stronger than those of copper, tin became very important. However, there was little tin to be found in western Asia—still the centre of the metal-working world. Mostly it was found in Europe, and the merchants of Troy, who brought their goods to Europe, began loading their boats with tin on their return journeys. In England, tin was discovered and mined in Cornwall and was a main export for a long time.

We have seen how the knowledge of metals spread from western Asia to Europe. The merchants' caravans carried the knowledge eastward as well. In India and China metal-workers flourished. The Chinese produced beautiful tall wine-storage vessels, cooking cauldrons, weapons and ornaments made of bronze.

The beautiful workmanship in bronze of the ancient Chinese artist-craftsmen

The great skill of the Egyptian metal-workers

The Chinese led the Ancient World in the use of bronze, and the Egyptians excelled in the working of gold. Of course, all the five metals then known were worked by the Egyptians, particularly bronze for the weapons used in their frequent wars. But it is their use of precious metals that is of most interest.

The enormous wealth of the Pharaohs provided endless opportunities for the Egyptian goldsmiths and silversmiths. At their disposal were their masters' vast hoards of precious metals; with these they produced work of the highest artistic and technical standards. Many masterpieces were buried with the Pharaohs, and excavation of their tombs has revealed Egyptian metal-work of great beauty produced some three thousand years ago.

These metal-workers were masters of the ancient craft of gold-beating, a process by which gold is beaten between skins until it is reduced to a very thin sheet. The Egyptians could produce sheets only one five-thousandth of an inch thick, and used them for gilding wooden statues and for other decorative purposes.

We gain some idea of their lavish use of gold and silver from the tomb of the young king Tutankhamen who died about 1,350 BC. When his tomb was opened in 1922, among the treasures revealed was a superb gold mask inlaid with stones, and in the middle of a number of gilt statues and shrines stood the king's coffin made of solid gold more than an inch thick.

Among all these lay some very small tools which today we would hardly notice. To the Egyptians they were the rarest and most valuable things in the tomb because they were made of *iron*—the sixth metal discovered by man.

16 Egyptian artists gilding statues for Tutankhamen's tomb, and (above) the gold mask of Tutankhamen

The importance of iron

The iron in Tutankhamen's tomb had not been found in Egypt but purchased from the Hittites, a powerful group of people living in Asia Minor and Syria—south of the Black Sea. They had discovered how to extract iron from iron-ore, and had kept the process a closely guarded secret.

Although often at war with the Egyptians, the Hittites willingly bartered their iron for gold. The Egyptians had to pay the Hittites in gold four times the weight of iron, or forty times its weight in silver. It is recorded that the Egyptians once deceived the Hittites with lumps of bronze covered with a thin layer of gold.

The smelting of iron was the most important metallurgical development since the potters found copper at the bottom of their kilns. Iron-ore is plentiful all over the world, therefore it may seem surprising that such a long time elapsed before iron was produced. The reason was that the furnaces used to smelt copper were not hot enough to produce iron. Many attempts had been made before the Hittites succeeded.

The Hittites kept their secret for over a century, but in 1,283 BC their country was over-run by invaders from the south. Many of the iron-workers fled to other countries, taking their secrets with them. Eventually their knowledge spread both east and west, and iron became cheap and plentiful. Its toughness, and the ease with which it could be worked when hot, made it superior to bronze in the manufacture of tools and weapons and other articles where strength was important.

A Hittite iron-worker

New skills and methods

Sometimes the early iron-workers, or *smiths*, accidentally produced a steel article instead of an iron one. Steel is iron with a small percentage of *carbon* in it. The carbon came from the fuel in the furnace in which the iron was heated. The smiths later learned from experience how to introduce this carbon when they wanted to produce steel.

Steel is stronger than iron, and can be made stronger still by *quenching*, which is the sudden cooling, in water or other fluids, from red-heat. However, steel becomes very brittle when made extremely hard, and as each smith used his own method the quality of the steel varied a great deal. Often a sword made by a poor smith snapped just when it was most needed.

In those days furnaces were not hot enough to melt iron completely. To extract the iron from the iron-ore, the ore was heated as much as possible (reducing the iron to a 'spongy' consistency) and then hammered. This forced the bits of rock and other impurities out, leaving the iron behind. Great skill and dexterity were required, especially as tongs had not been invented and the hot metal was handled with green sticks.

Meanwhile production of the earlier metals continued to expand. Gold was no longer just picked up from streams in lumps; it was mined, or extracted from streams in the form of dust. One interesting way of filtering the gold-dust out of the water was by using a sheep's fleece in a trough. The gold particles were caught in the wool which was then burnt, leaving the gold behind. The legend of Jason and the Golden Fleece probably derives from this process.

⚬ A sheep's fleece used to filter gold dust from water

The discovery of mercury and zinc

After iron, two more metals were discovered. The first was *mercury*, the liquid metal now used in thermometers. It was discovered about 200 BC, possibly in Spain. It is sometimes called 'quicksilver' because 'quick' means 'alive', and mercury looks like silver.

The second metal was *zinc*, which was used to produce an important alloy in combination with copper. This alloy was *brass*, a hard-wearing, yellow metal which was valued more than bronze. The exact date of discovery is uncertain but it was probably about 200 BC. Brass is often mentioned in the Old Testament, most of which was written before zinc was discovered and therefore when there could not have been any brass. The biblical metal must have been either bronze or copper, and the word 'brass' the result of a translator's error at some time.

The discovery of mercury and zinc brought the number of known basic metals to eight.

Over the centuries, interest in the known metals had increased greatly. In the times of the Pharaohs, considerable advances were made in chemistry and metallurgy. About 500 BC an astonishing theory was put forward by a Greek named Democritus; by sheer reasoning he arrived at the theory that all matter consists of whirling atoms—an opinion still held today.

A less admirable idea spread by the Greeks was that gold might be made from base metals (iron, lead, etc.). This started the biggest wild-goose chase in history. People who tried to make gold were called *alchemists*. They were serious scientists and in the course of their experiments made some useful discoveries. But their main aim—to make gold—was doomed to failure. Gold is a basic metal.

Metals in Roman times

The Romans were superb engineers and administrators as well as a great military power. Their empire spread far and wide, and the mining and working of metal was well organised in all the countries over which they ruled. By law, all metal found in occupied countries belonged to Rome.

The army required iron, bronze and brass for its weapons and armour. Even gold was used to make military standards visible from a distance.

In their domestic life, the Romans used metal extensively and skilfully. Their saw-blades could cut through metal as easily as a modern hack-saw. They drew bronze wire as fine as 1/50th of an inch, twisting many strands together to make a cable, and they excelled in joining metals by welding (heating and hammering together) and soldering.

Brass, which was then a very new metal, was used for coinage. At first the Romans used 'bar' money, but later introduced round coins. The coins were stamped with a hard metal *die* which left an impression of the design and lettering.

Pewter, an alloy of lead and tin, was used to make cups and dishes.

Some Roman aqueducts still stand today, and were part of their brilliantly engineered, irrigation canal systems. These aqueducts were lined with lead because it did not rust. Many thousands of tons were used in a single aqueduct. So much lead was used in water supply systems that eventually the Romans suffered some lead-poisoning.

The most important metal to the Romans was gold. They acquired hundreds of millions of pounds worth, and spent much of it on the luxuries desired by the people of Rome.

The coming of the Vikings

After the fall of the Roman Empire in 476 AD, there was little progress in the working of metals for many years. Iron-smelting, tin and lead mining, and the general metal-working developed by the Romans in occupied countries almost ceased. What metal-work was still carried on was of poor quality.

Then, about 800 AD, a new power entered northern Europe—the Vikings. These men from the north, Norsemen, were great seafarers and fighters. They owed much of their success to their skill with metal. Their swords were much longer and stronger than those used by the Romans, and with these they won their battles.

In those days it was difficult to make good swords because of the lack of furnaces hot enough to melt iron sufficiently to treat it with carbon and turn it into steel. All that could be done was to heat the iron in charcoal, which is rich in carbon. Some carbon from the charcoal found its way into the metal and hardened it on the surface, like the crust on a loaf.

The swordmakers built up their blades by taking a number of thin strips, which had been hardened on their surfaces, and twisting them together in various patterns (one of which is shown opposite). The metal was then reheated and hammered (forged) until it became a solid piece with hardened strips running right through the blade. As well as making the blade strong, this method also created an interesting wavy pattern on the metal.

A Viking invasion. (Below) Their sword blades were built up of many thin strips, heated and hammered together

The Crusades

In 1066 the Norman conquest of Britain brought England into closer relationship with France and other European countries. When the Crusades started, English warriors joined their continental brethren in trying to gain control of Jerusalem.

The fall of Rome did not affect life in eastern countries in quite the same way that it had done in Europe. The crusaders, coming from rough, comfortless homes —even those of them who lived in castles—were astonished by the luxury and elegance of the eastern countries. They longed to imitate the splendid architecture they saw, and they found that the eastern metal-workers were superior to their own. The Muslims did not have any additional new metals, but possessed greater technical skill in the arts of forging, casting and working the known ones.

There is a legend which tells of a meeting in the desert between Richard the Lion Heart and Saladin, the Muslim leader. Comparing weapons, Richard smashed through an iron bar with his mighty two-handed sword. In reply, Saladin flicked a silk scarf into the air and sliced it in half with his razor-sharp scimitar. Though not a true story, this legend makes a very apt comment on the metallurgical superiority of the Muslims' swordsmiths. To retain such a sharp edge, Saladin's blade must have been made of far superior metal.

The Muslims had a special method of making sword-blades which they had learned from India, hundreds of years before the Crusades. Blades made by this technique were known as Damascene. As well as being very strong, they had beautiful surfaces which shimmered like watered silk.

Water-power and metal-working

The Middle Ages saw the first steps towards mechanisation in the metal industry. Water-wheels had long been used for grinding corn and in the making of cloth, and over five thousand mills were listed in the Domesday Book. Large water-wheels could now be made to drive mechanical hammers and work the bellows of furnaces. This dependence on water-power had the effect of moving the iron industries into definite areas. Three things were needed in the locality of the works, water to drive the wheels, forests to provide fuel, and—of course—iron-ore.

In England one such district which supplied these needs was Sussex, which also had the advantage of a good market not far away in London. The area is rich in iron-ore, and Sussex churches sometimes reveal the iron in the stone of which they are built by 'weeping' rust (iron oxide) down the sides of a tower. To increase the efficiency of the water-wheels, 'hammer-ponds' were dug, and the remains of these can still be seen today.

The way in which the water-wheel drove the hammer is shown in the picture opposite. The hammer, which weighed about two hundredweight, was lifted by the projections on the drum until it slipped off and fell on to the anvil, assisted downwards by a beam of springy wood above. It could deliver about a hundred blows a minute, and this speed was very important when forging (shaping hot metal by hammering), because the iron cooled rapidly and had to be heated repeatedly.

It was in Sussex that the first cast-iron cannon was made, and the industry there was famous for beautiful cast-iron fire-backs.

(Above) **Iron-content of stones stains the walls of a Sussex church**
(Below) **A water-powered hammer**

Water-wheel **1** drives drum **2**. Knobs **3** raise hammer **4** till it drops back onto anvil **5**. Flexible ash spring **6** adds speed to falling hammer.

The first blast-furnaces

So far, no furnace in Europe had been hot enough to melt iron to a liquid state. All that could be produced was a 'spongy' mass from which impurities had to be hammered out. However, design of furnaces improved over the centuries, and about the year 1400 very efficient *blast-furnaces* were introduced by the Germans. They had found that a blast of air from water-powered bellows increased the temperature, though the iron still did not liquify. It became soft and spongy, worked its way down through the burning charcoal, and collected at the bottom of the furnace.

Furnaces were usually built about ten or fifteen feet high, but to economise on fuel a new one was built thirty feet high. Although the internal temperature in this was no higher, the iron arrived at the bottom in a completely liquid state. Not only could the metal be run off into moulds, but many of the impurities (which had previously to be hammered out) separated automatically from the melted iron. The reason for this tremendous stride in metallurgy was simply the height of the furnace. The soft 'sponge' iron took so long to seep down through the charcoal that it absorbed a great deal of carbon. It became *carburised*, and as the melting point of carburised iron is 350°C less than 'sponge' iron, it became liquid.

An interesting machine for making wire is shown opposite. A crank was driven by a water-wheel, and attached to the crank by a rope was a pair of pincers which moved back and forth as the crank rotated. Metal rod was pulled through a series of holes in an iron plate, each hole smaller than the previous one, until a thin wire was achieved. The pincers were closed on the wire each time the crank moved forwards and as it moved back it dragged the wire through the hole in the plate.

(Above) A blast-furnace with water-powered bellows
(Below) Water-power being used to draw wire

Water-wheel **1** drives cams **2** which close bellows **3**, Weight **4** opens bellows. Air passes through pipes to furnace via holes **5**. Lining **6** is broken to extract iron bloom.

The alchemists

Earlier in this book we learned how early alchemists tried to turn other metals into gold. Centuries had passed since the Greeks started this search for quick wealth, and greed still urged on the alchemists to make their endless experiments.

Between 1100 and 1400 some alchemists were paying attention to another form of so-called science. This was to find the 'elixir of life', which would make men live for ever. Another thing they hoped to discover was the 'Philosopher's Stone', which would not only cure all diseases but also convert metals such as copper into gold. The experiments the alchemists made were sometimes very elaborate. Some put the metals through a hundred purifying processes and added a great deal of so-called magic as well. Of course, all these efforts came to nothing, but the alchemists were convinced that they would succeed and plodded on until about the seventeenth century. Even the great Sir Isaac Newton had some faith in alchemy.

Although some scientific knowledge was acquired during the course of these experiments, the basic idea behind them was not to enrich the minds of men with a store of knowledge but to enrich the alchemists themselves with a store of gold. Dishonest people became interested and decided that it was unnecessary to make real gold—but merely something that looked like it. Soon these people, who were called 'Puffers', were selling false gold to the credulous. Laws and dire penalties were devised to stop them, but they continued to operate on an international scale until the Royal Mints were established. Nothing could then be valued as real gold unless it had the 'hallmark' of the Royal Mint on it.

　　　An alchemist tries to turn base metal into gold

The mining of metals

All but a few metals are extracted from the ground in the form of ores, and the method of extracting them is called *mining*. If the ore lies on, or close to, the surface of the earth it can be collected simply by using power-shovels to scoop it up. This method is called *surface-mining*. Other ores are found at the bottom of rivers and lakes, these are *alluvial-deposits*, and are collected by dredging and sifting. A gold prospector *pans* for gold in alluvial deposits by washing gravel through a felt-lined box. The gold clings to the felt just as it did to the golden fleece mentioned earlier in this book. Tin is sometimes panned in this way but on a large scale, using huge dredgers. *Underground* deposits are reached by digging a shaft down to the level of the ore, and then digging horizontal tunnels or *galleries*.

Throughout the history of metals the technical methods of mining have improved. In the early days of mining one of the most difficult problems was that of ventilation, as miners cannot live without fresh air. Ventilation shafts were dug to create a natural draught, and big bellows were driven by horses or water-wheels.

The picture opposite is based on details from a mediaeval painting in a church in Saxony (Germany), a district rich in silver ores. Each of the shafts had a little hut built over it to keep the rain out. A miner is going down with a 'ladder-peg' lamp on his head, whilst two miners wearing knee-caps made of leather, winch up ore in a bucket. Another man breaks the ore into smaller pieces ready for carting away for smelting and processing.

Metal-mining in the Middle Ages

Platinum and antimony

When Christopher Columbus discovered the Americas in 1492, the Queen of Spain claimed the land and its inhabitants as her property and demanded the greater part of any treasure that was found.

Spanish expeditions soon followed, and though they are much criticised for their cruelty, greed and treachery, the military achievements of these 'Conquistadores' were remarkable. First they conquered Mexico and took away its valuable treasures. Seeking more land and wealth they invaded Peru, home of the Incas. Here they murdered the king and stole his vast hoard of gold—probably the greatest in the world. The natives were enslaved and set to work to win more gold. Later the Spanish conquered Chile and Bolivia, both of these countries being rich in precious metals, particularly silver.

To the metallurgist, the most exciting discovery made by the Spaniards was the finding of *platinum* in the silver mines of Mexico. At that time the new metal was regarded as more of a nuisance than of value. It could not be melted by any known method, though it was possible to make a very realistic imitation gold from it. Later it joined the group of precious metals and is now used for jewellery and in industry. Its high melting point makes it suitable for electrical contacts where the heat of sparks would melt other metals. In the chemical industries its resistance to corrosion is of great value.

Methods of producing *antimony* were discovered in Europe at this time. The alchemists called it 'the wolf of metals' because they thought it devoured all metals but gold. It is used to harden lead for such purposes as electric battery plates and printer's 'type metal'.

Iron-smelting without charcoal

By about the year 1600, iron production in Britain was beginning to suffer from lack of fuel. For 3,000 years all iron-smelting, both here and abroad, had been done with charcoal. Charcoal is partly-burned wood. In Britain, timber was running short and it was impossible for the iron-makers to equal the output of a country such as Sweden, where timber was abundant.

Fortunately for Britain a Quaker, Abraham Darby, found a way to do without charcoal altogether. In his iron factory at Coalbrookdale, Shropshire, he made many experiments using coke, and finally succeeded. There were technical difficulties to overcome, and at first Darby kept the process secret for the benefit of his family. Later his methods were adopted throughout Europe. No longer dependant on dwindling forests, Britain regained her position as a leading iron producer.

Abraham Darby died in 1717, and his ironworks were managed by his son, Abraham Darby II. In turn he was followed by *his* son, also called Abraham Darby. Abraham Darby III built a noble testimonial to the work of the Darby family. This is the iron bridge erected in 1779 to span the River Severn near the ironworks at Coalbrookdale. It was built of prefabricated parts made in the Darbys' factory, and was the first of its kind in the world. The bridge was erected in the amazingly short time of three months, without accident and without obstructing the busy river traffic. It has a span of about 100 feet and gave 150 years of service before being closed to traffic in 1934. It is a fine monument to British enterprise and well worth going to see.

The vast growth of the iron and steel industry

When James Watt invented the steam engine in the latter part of the eighteenth century, the whole industrial scene changed. Steam power made possible the 'Industrial Revolution' in Britain. Vast quantities of metal were needed for the railways pioneered by the Stevensons, and the huge iron ships and bridges of Brunel. In Sheffield, the centre of the iron and steel industry, the output of metals multiplied fifty times in thirty-five years.

During this expansion, improved tools were invented for use in the factories and many steam-powered tools were invented and developed. One of the most famous of these tools was the steam-hammer designed by James Nasmyth about 1830. It was used to forge the huge shafts and plates required in the ships of the time, and could be accurately controlled to give heavy blows or light taps. In fact, to impress visitors to the foundry an egg was placed on the anvil and cracked by the hammer without breaking the egg-shell. Other machine-tools invented and developed included the rolling-mill which could roll metal, either hot or cold, into thin sheets. Another device was the extrusion-press, which forced hot metal through a hole like tooth-paste from a tube. Railway lines could be made in this way, the hole in the press being suitably shaped to the section of the railway-line.

These tremendous advances in engineering were matched by improvements in the quality of metals, and the metallurgists were as active and successful as the engineers. Between 1750 and 1850 no less than thirty-five more metals were discovered. Many of these were unimportant but three were outstanding, *nickel*, *cobalt* and *manganese*, the latter to play a vital part in steel production.

More progress in steel production

Iron coming from a blast furnace is called *pig-iron*, and still contains many impurities which have to be removed before it can be converted into steel. During the Industrial Revolution the demand for steel was so great that better and quicker methods of producing it became necessary. A big step forward was made with the invention of the 'Bessemer Converter'. Henry Bessemer's idea was that the impurities would be burned away if air was blown through molten pig-iron.

An experimental vessel to contain 7 cwts. of molten pig-iron was set up in Bessemer's factory. Air pipes led into the bottom of the vessel, and when the air was turned on huge flames and showers of sparks shot out of the mouth of the converter, followed by spurts of molten metal and slag. Bessemer and his workers could only retreat and hope for the best. They could not turn off the air because the air-valve had been placed too near to the converter. However, after ten minutes the eruption subsided and it was found that the iron was free of impurities.

The new process was widely adopted, and converters were built which could purify several tons of pig-iron in half-an-hour—an enormous improvement on previous methods. The Bessemer 'blow', with flames shooting high into the air, is one of the most dramatic sights in steel manufacture.

Other methods followed, the Siemens 'open hearth' furnaces were slower than the Bessemer converter but gave better control. 'Electric arc' furnaces were introduced later.

Two metals, *manganese* and *chromium*, discovered in 1774, were to play an important role in steel manufacture. Small quantities of manganese in steel adds greatly to its strength. Chromium is used in the manufacture of stainless steel.

A Bessemer Converter 'blow'

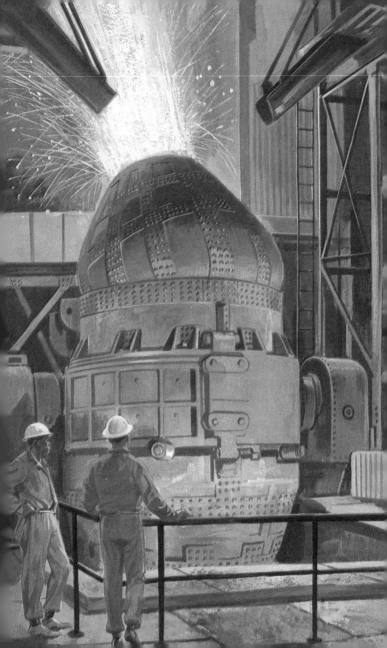

The importance of aluminium

So much *aluminium* is used today that it is hard to believe that a little over a hundred years ago it was a 'precious' metal, just as iron was to the Egyptians in the days of Tutankhamen. Yet of all the metals in the Earth's crust, aluminium is more plentiful than any other. It is never found 'free' and great problems had to be solved before it could be extracted from its ores.

Napoleon III encouraged scientists working on the new metal because he thought it would lighten the equipment of his troops. In 1854 an aluminium medal was presented to the Emperor, and a small bar of the precious metal was placed among the French Crown Jewels.

Humphrey Davy, the great British scientist, tried to produce aluminium but failed. The problem was finally solved by two scientists, one living in France and the other in the U.S.A. Neither knew anything of the other or his work, yet both used the same method to produce aluminium, and succeeded within a few weeks of one another.

Aluminium was then produced on a commercial scale, and the price fell rapidly. Today an aluminium medal would be more in place in a Christmas cracker than on an emperor's chest. Enormous quantities are used for many things, from milk-bottle tops to Jumbo-jets. It is so light that a man can carry a heavy looking aluminium structure quite easily. It is not very strong but *duralumin* alloys, mainly made by adding magnesium to aluminium, are very suitable for aircraft structures where great strength is necessary.

Because of the lightness of aluminium, a structure of great strength can easily be carried

Radio-active metals

During the last two hundred years many new metals have been discovered, and altogether seventy metallic elements are now known. Many of these metals are of interest only to scientists.

You will remember that earlier in this book we told of the Greek, Democritus, who stated that matter consisted of atoms in motion. During the latter part of the nineteenth century, scientists became very interested in the nature and structure of atoms. A great deal of experimental work was carried out and many important discoveries made. Röntgen discovered X-rays in 1895, and in 1896 Henri Becquerel investigated the radio-active properties of *uranium*. Radio-active metals such as *uranium* and *radium* give out a stream of active rays. Marie and Pierre Curie* discovered the metal *radium* in the same ore (pitchblende) that contained uranium.

Using uranium, scientists conducted experiments in 1936 to 'split' the atom. This splitting of the uranium atom released such tremendous forces that it was at first kept secret due to its terrible potential in warfare. Tragically, it was later used for that purpose during the Second World War, when the first atomic bomb was exploded. Since the war, many more atomic bombs have been exploded experimentally.

Fortunately the tremendous forces released by atom-splitting can be controlled and the energy released gradually. In this way they can be used to generate heat to drive power-stations and therefore benefit mankind.

*See the Ladybird book (Madame Curie).

(Above) Radio-active pitchblende being mined in Africa
(Below) Left: An atomic power-station
Right: Scientists watch an atomic explosion
many miles away

Metals in our modern age

Today, metallurgy is a highly complex science, and the tremendous advances in technology during this century have made necessary the development of many new alloys. For example, when jet aircraft engines were introduced, special alloys such as those using nickel and chromium were developed to withstand the high temperatures involved. The enormous heat in space-ship rocket engines presented further formidable problems to the metallurgists.

Very few metals are still used in their pure state. Copper of high purity is of great value in electrical engineering, but most metals we use are alloys, developed by the metallurgist to suit each special requirement. Thus a 'high-speed' steel cutting tool for use on a lathe can contain percentages of tungsten and chromium. Altogether about four thousand such different alloys are recognised and used today for various purposes.

Man's curiosity is boundless. Having solved the countless problems involved in placing man and machine on the moon, almost his first act was to analyse its composition. Samples of moon-rock were brought back to Earth by the Americans for analysis.

The Russians placed a robot laboratory on the moon itself. This robot, Lunokhod II, took up samples at frequent stopping places and transmitted information back to Earth by radio. Aluminium, iron, titanium, magnesium, potassium and calcium have been found in this way. The advantage of such a device as Lunokhod lies in the possibility of putting it onto some remote and inhospitable planet where men cannot at present hope to set foot. There, perhaps, might be found some entirely new and unknown metal.

A Lunokhod II at work on the moon

A list of the more important metals and their uses

ALUMINIUM   A very light, silvery-coloured metal.   It is rather soft, but becomes as strong as steel when alloyed with magnesium, copper, etc.   A good conductor of heat and electricity.

ANTIMONY   A hard, brittle metal used in alloys of lead.

CADMIUM   Used to electro-plate iron for rust protection. Also used for control rods in the atomic reactors of nuclear power stations.

CHROMIUM   Used to give a shiny plating to other metals, and used in alloys of steel to produce stainless steel.

COBALT   Used in the manufacture of steel cutting-tools. It also produces the blue used in pottery such as the famous 'Sevres' products.

COPPER   One of the few metals used 'pure'.   It is an excellent conductor of electricity and is used for wires and cables.

GERMANIUM   Crystals of this metal are used for the transistors in transistor radio circuits.

GOLD   A very soft, precious metal which does not tarnish or corrode.   Gold is alloyed with silver or copper to give sufficient strength to some objects.

IRON   The most useful of all metals.   Iron oxidises in water (rusts).   Alloyed with carbon it produces steel.